How to Draw
ZOO ANIMALS

Learn to draw **20** wild creatures, step by easy step, shape by simple shape!

Illustrated by Diana Fisher

GETTING STARTED

When you look closely at the drawings in this book, you'll notice that they're made up of basic shapes, such as circles, triangles, and rectangles. To draw any wild kingdom animals, just start with simple shapes as you see here. It's easy and fun!

CIRCLES are great for drawing heads, chests, and hips.

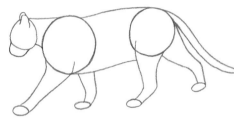 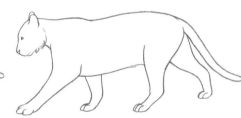

OVALS are good for drawing animals' bodies.

TRIANGLES are often best for drawing beaks, ears, and hooves.

TIPS

There's more than one way to bring your animal pals to life on paper—you can use crayons, markers, or pencils. Just be sure you have plenty of natural hues, such as black and shades of brown, plus yellow, orange, red, and green.

Pencils

Crayons

Markers

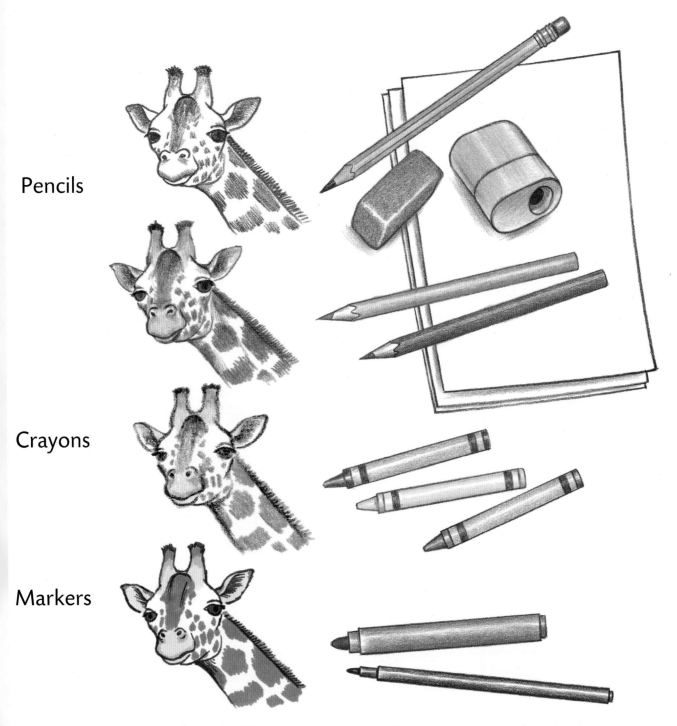

GIANT PANDA

In china the barrel-shaped panda is called *baixiong* ("white bear"), but the black markings give this animal a two-toned look.

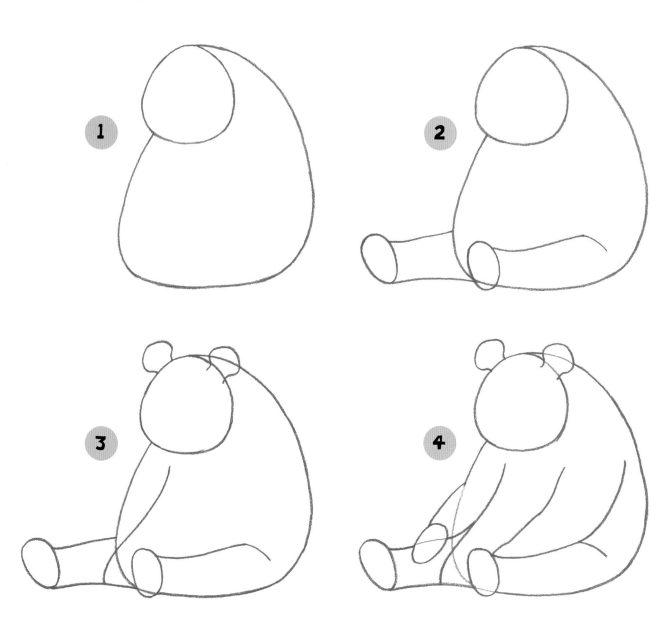

FUN FACT

The giant panda has a very limited diet—it survives almost entirely on bamboo! It eats the shoots of this grasslike plant in the spring, leaves in the summer, and stems in the winter.

5

6

At Risk

As of 2016, the giant panda is no longer considered an endangered species.

7

POLAR BEAR

The cuddly-looking polar bear has a large, round, furry body—but this cutie hunts and devours seals, walruses, and even whales!

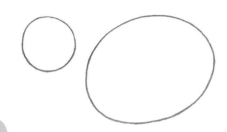

1

2

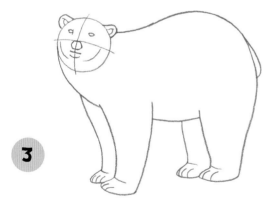

3

4

At Risk

The population of polar bears decreases every day. Efforts must be made to save the bear and its Arctic home to prevent extinction.

5

CHEETAH

with its long, powerful legs; lean, muscular body; and stylish, spotted coat, you might say the cheetah is a hunter "dressed to kill"!

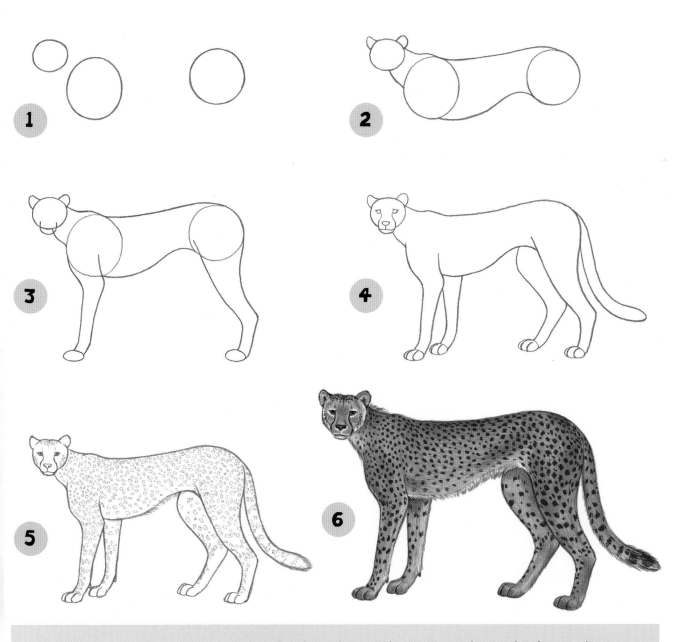

FUN FACT

Sure, the cheetah is quick—it can reach speeds of more than 60 mph (97 kph), making it the fastest animal in the world. But this big cat can maintain its top speed only for short bursts. After 10–12 seconds of running, the cheetah begins to overheat.

ELEPHANT

One of the largest beasts of the animal kingdom, an African elephant has a thick trunk, big legs, long tusks, and giant ears!

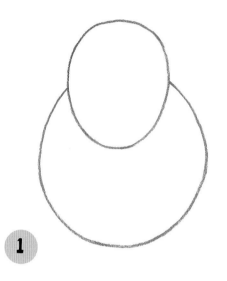

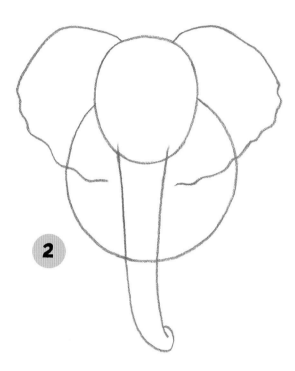

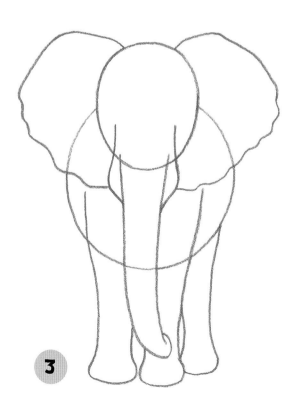

FUN FACT

The elephant is known for its great memory—but why? One reason is the elephant has an enormous brain! Weighing in at around 12 pounds (5.4 kg), it's the largest and heaviest mammal brain. (The human brain weighs only about 3 pounds [1.3 kg].)

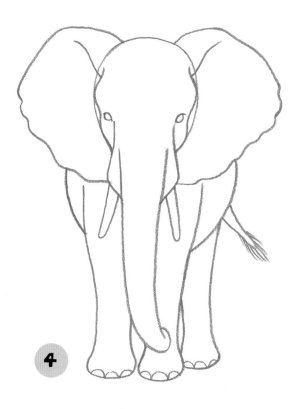

4

5

6

At Risk

The African elephant has a very high chance of becoming extinct in the next 20 years.

TIGER

Every big cat has a large head and rounded ears.
But a tiger also has camouflaging stripes
that help this stand-out cat blend in!

FUN FACT

A tiger usually eats about 15–35 pounds (6.8–16 kg) of meat per feeding, dining on deer, pigs, cattle, monkeys, birds, reptiles, and even fish. And when it's really hungry, a tiger can eat up to 90 pounds (40.8 kg) of meat in one meal!

TOUCAN

It's hard to ignore the keel-billed toucan's vibrant beak! It's almost as long as the bird's body.

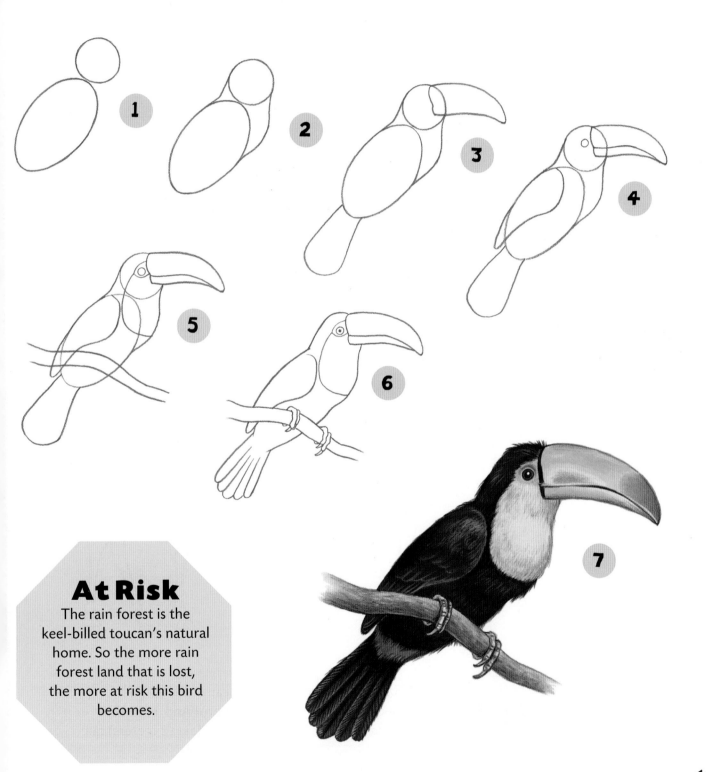

At Risk

The rain forest is the keel-billed toucan's natural home. So the more rain forest land that is lost, the more at risk this bird becomes.

GIRAFFE

With its lanky legs and long neck, the towering giraffe rises above the competition to claim the title of "tallest animal on Earth."

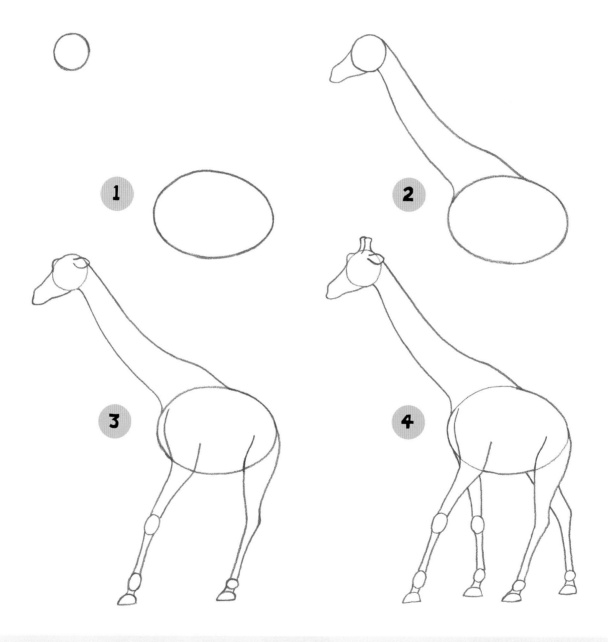

FUN FACT

A baby giraffe, called a "calf," can stand up on its own about 20 minutes after it's born! And, at birth, a giraffe calf already measures about 6½ feet (2 meters) tall!

5

6

At Risk

The giraffe is at risk of extinction because humans continue to damage and destroy the African savannas and grasslands where it lives.

7

8

TAPIR

High Risk

What's black and white with a long curved snout? The Malayan tapir! This "living fossil" has looked exactly the same for 30 million years!

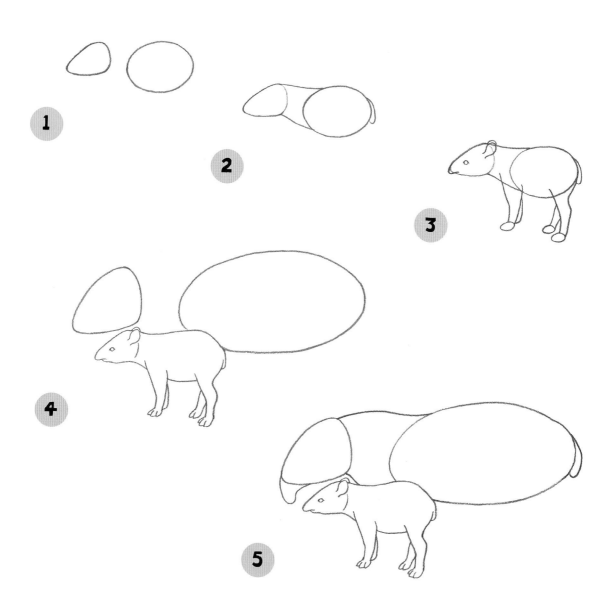

FUN FACT

Every tapir is born with spots and stripes. This camouflage pattern protects the young tapir from predators, helping it blend in with vegetation. The "broken" pattern of the adult Malayan tapir also acts as camouflage.

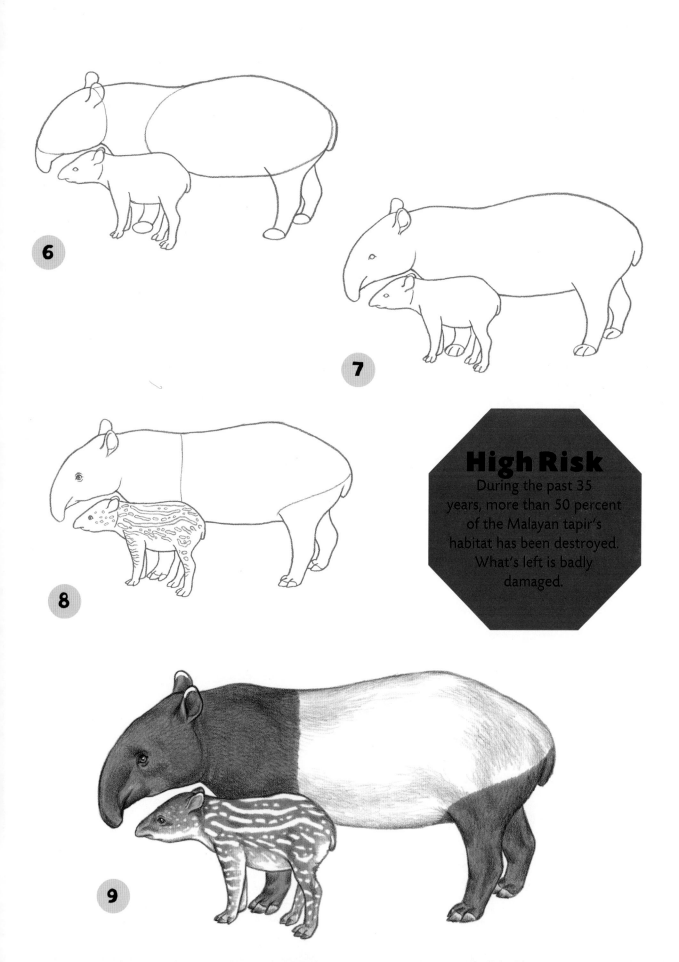

High Risk
During the past 35 years, more than 50 percent of the Malayan tapir's habitat has been destroyed. What's left is badly damaged.

HIPPOPOTAMUS

"Massive" is a good start for describing this
round, hulking beast! A full-grown hippo can
weigh up to 1½ tons (1,360 kilograms).

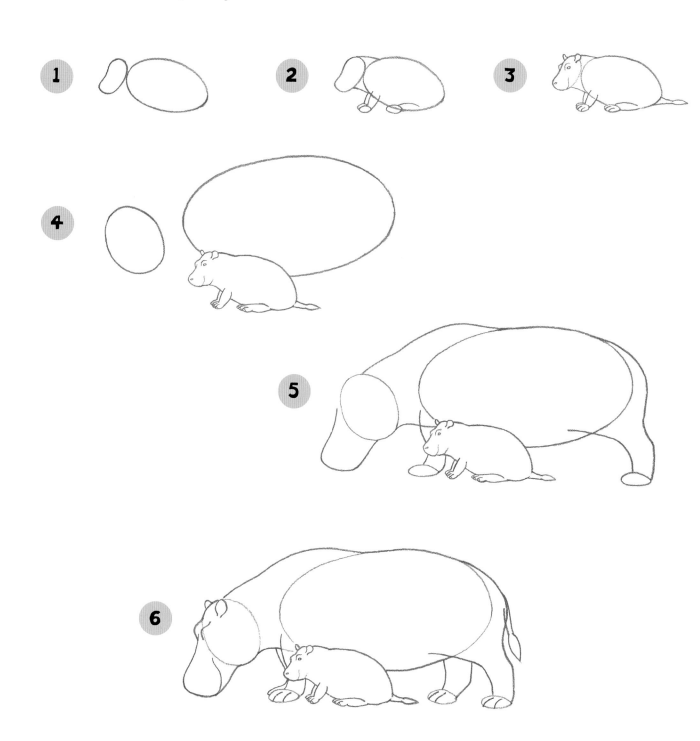

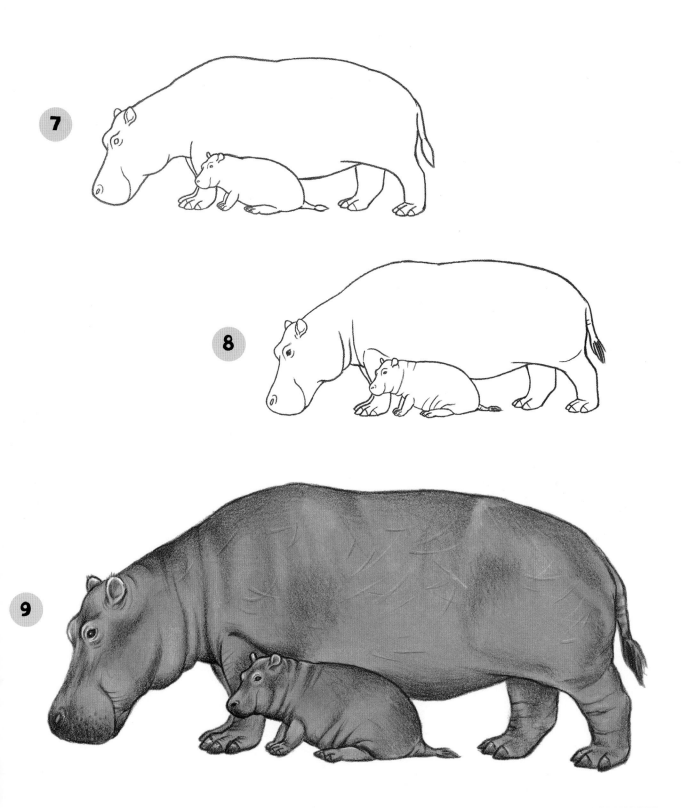

FUN FACT

The common hippo is amphibious, meaning it lives both on land and in water. Its webbed toes and high-placed eyes, ears, and nostrils allow it to easily take a breath, a look, and a listen while spending long periods of time underwater.

KANGAROO

with a thick, powerful tail, strong hind legs, and huge rear feet, you can identify the kangaroo from a hop, skip, and a jump away!

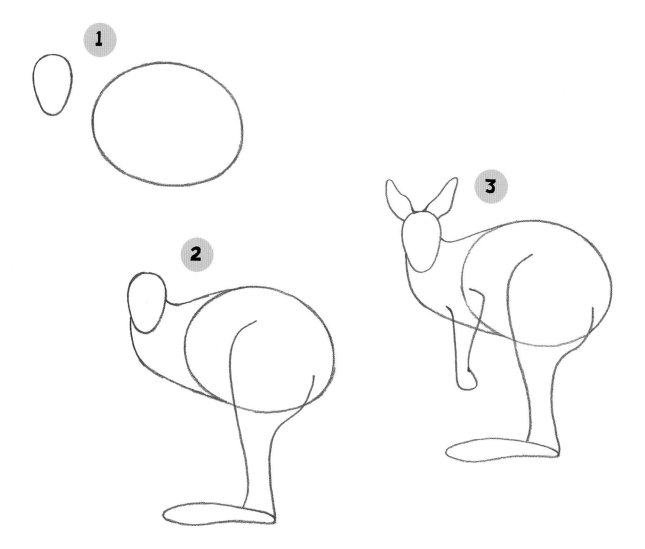

FUN FACT

For male kangaroos, kick boxing isn't a sport; it's a way of life. When fighting over mates, food, and resting spots, kangaroos will lock arms with each other, lean on their tails, and kick. The first kangaroo to get pushed over loses.

Low Risk

There are a lot of kangaroos in the wild in Australia, and their habitat isn't in danger. That places the kangaroo at low risk of extinction.

KOALA

This soft, woolly tree-dweller suspends
its short, round body by clinging to eucalyptus
trees—both its home and its food.

At Risk
In Australia, koala
habitats are frequently
destroyed to create homes and
roads for people. And koalas
are often victims
of forest fires.

LEMUR

Although its long, curving tail is the ring-tailed lemur's most striking feature, this animal is also known for its graceful, catlike posture.

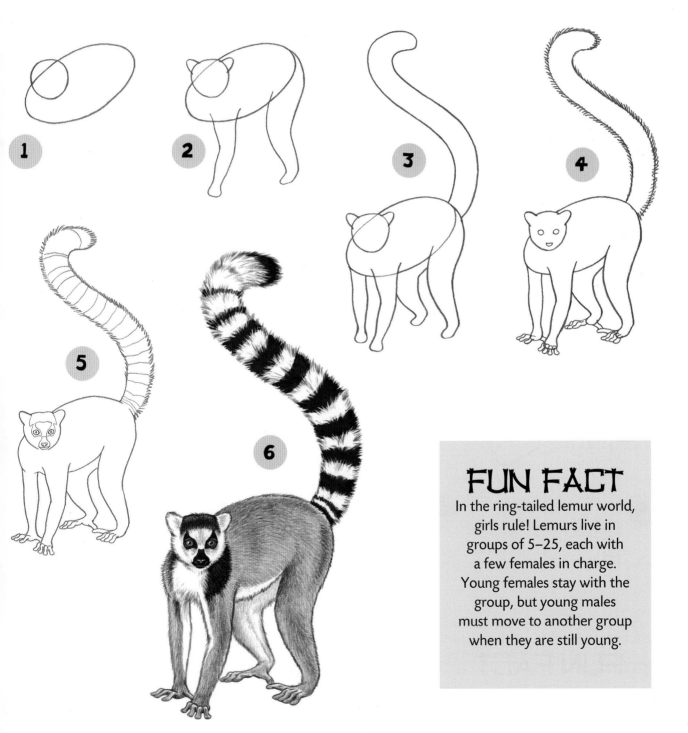

FUN FACT

In the ring-tailed lemur world, girls rule! Lemurs live in groups of 5–25, each with a few females in charge. Young females stay with the group, but young males must move to another group when they are still young.

SPIDER MONKEY

Black-handed spider monkeys are small and thin. Their hands, feet, and heads are black, and black masks frame their round eyes.

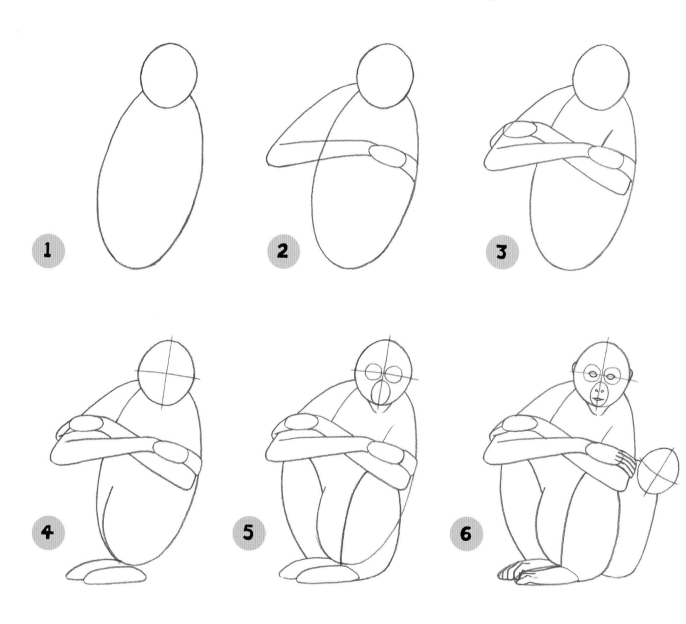

FUN FACT

This monkey gets its name from its long, spidery limbs—all five of them! The spider monkey's tail is as long and as strong as its arms and legs. And the tail's hairless tip makes it easier for the monkey to tightly grasp branches or food!

High Risk

The black-handed spider monkey has lost about 70 percent of its Central American habitat.

7

8

9

10

KOMODO DRAGON

Don't let its draggin' belly fool you—the large, wrinkled, prehistoric-looking Komodo dragon is a swift runner and a fast climber.

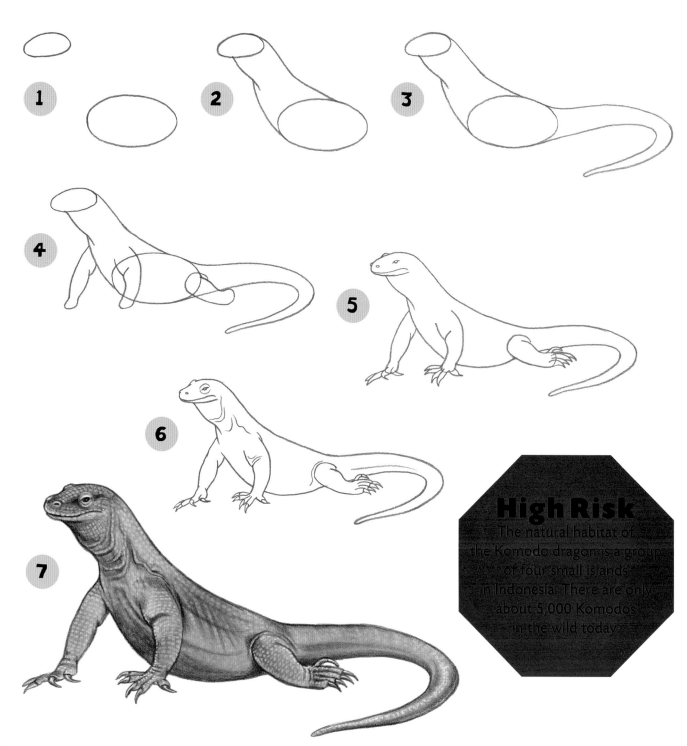

High Risk
The natural habitat of the Komodo dragon is a group of four small islands in Indonesia. There are only about 5,000 Komodos in the wild today.

ARMADILLO

Oddly enough, the "nine-banded" armadillo can have from 8 to 10 bands around its body, making its tough exterior more flexible.

1

2

3

4

FUN FACT

Many mammals give birth to multiple young, but only the nine-banded armadillo regularly produces them all from a single egg. The female nine-banded armadillo always gives birth to quadruplets—that's four identical baby armadillos.

5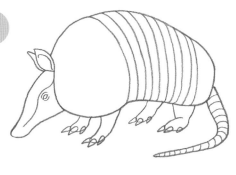

6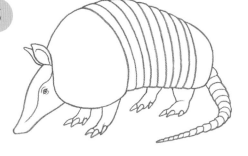

7

RHINOCEROS

The short legs of this white rhino support its bulky body, and it uses its two curved, triangular-shaped horns to dig food and defend itself!

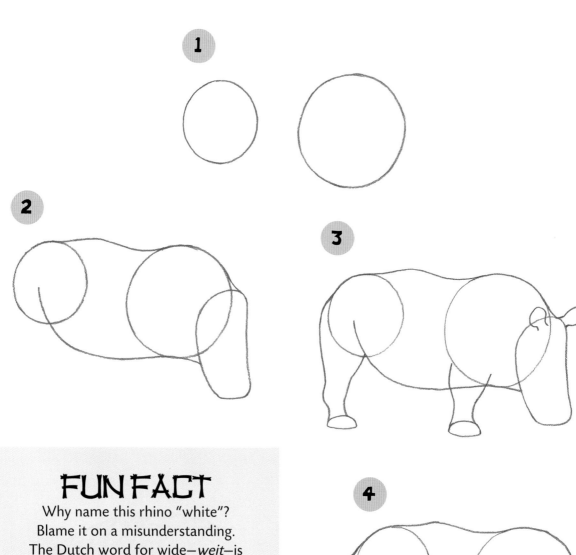

FUN FACT

Why name this rhino "white"? Blame it on a misunderstanding. The Dutch word for wide—*weit*—is pronounced "white." Weit was meant to describe the rhino's wide, square muzzle—not its skin. It's no coincidence that this animal is also called the "square-lipped" rhino.

5

6

7

PLATYPUS

It may have a duck's bill and webbed feet, but the platypus's flat tail and velvety, waterproof coat are all its own!

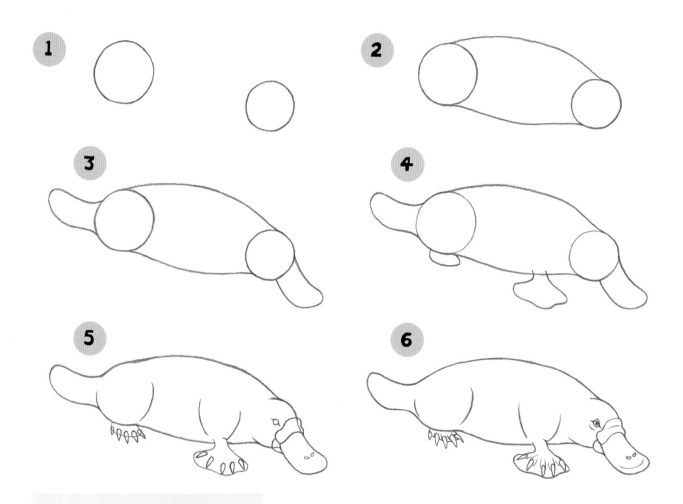

FUN FACT

The platypus isn't psychic, but it does have ESP—extra sensory perception! In addition to using sight, sound, taste, smell, and touch, the platypus can sense tiny electrical signals with its snout, helping it find food underwater.

ORANGUTAN

Every orangutan has a bare face, round eyes, and small ears, but only the male has large, round cheek pads and a long, hairy beard.

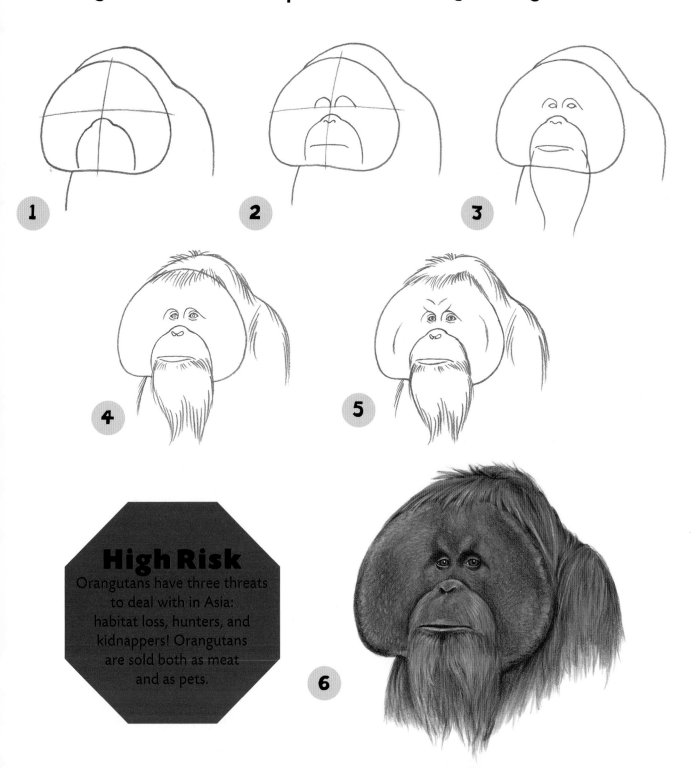

1

2

3

4

5

High Risk
Orangutans have three threats to deal with in Asia: habitat loss, hunters, and kidnappers! Orangutans are sold both as meat and as pets.

6

OKAPI

Its stripes make the okapi look like a zebra, but this tall, two-toned animal has the long legs and flexible neck of a giraffe.

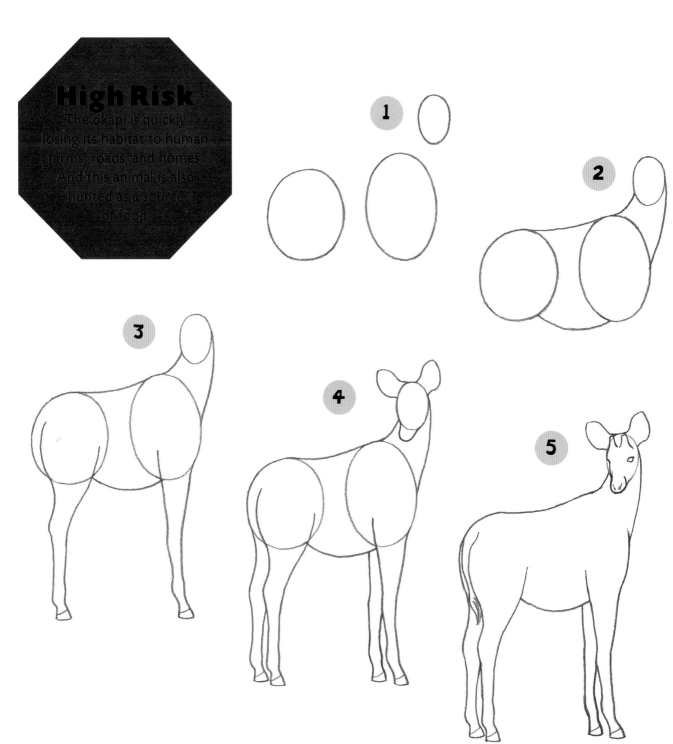

High Risk
The okapi is quickly losing its habitat to human farms, roads, and homes. And this animal is also hunted as a source of food.

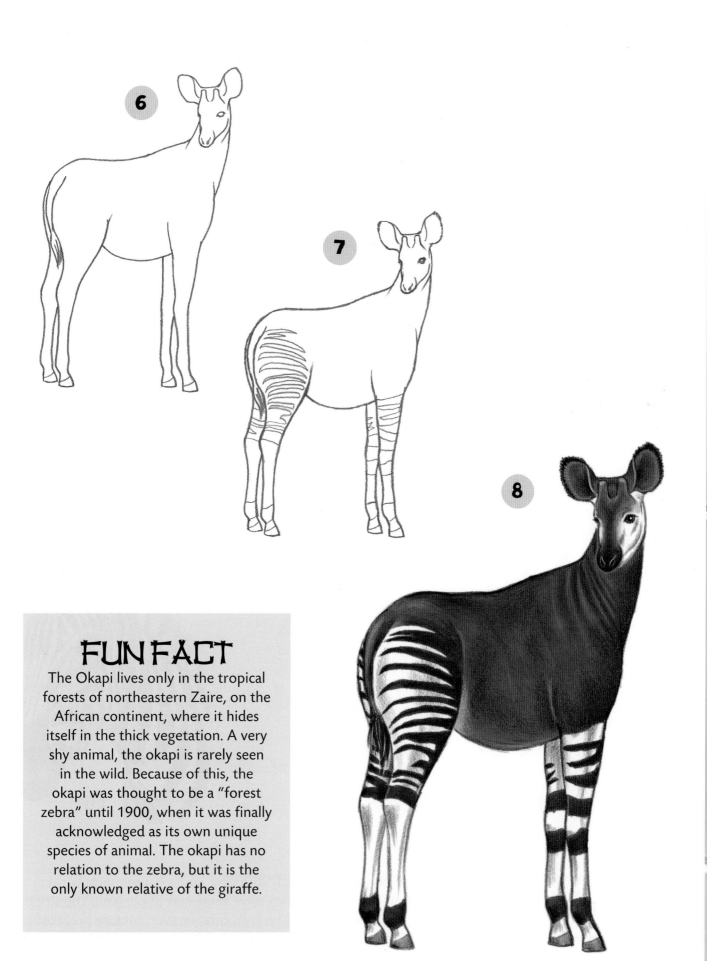

FUN FACT

The Okapi lives only in the tropical forests of northeastern Zaire, on the African continent, where it hides itself in the thick vegetation. A very shy animal, the okapi is rarely seen in the wild. Because of this, the okapi was thought to be a "forest zebra" until 1900, when it was finally acknowledged as its own unique species of animal. The okapi has no relation to the zebra, but it is the only known relative of the giraffe.

ZEBRA

From its black muzzle to the tips of its long ears, the zebra's face is covered in narrow stripes; its body and mane have broader stripes.

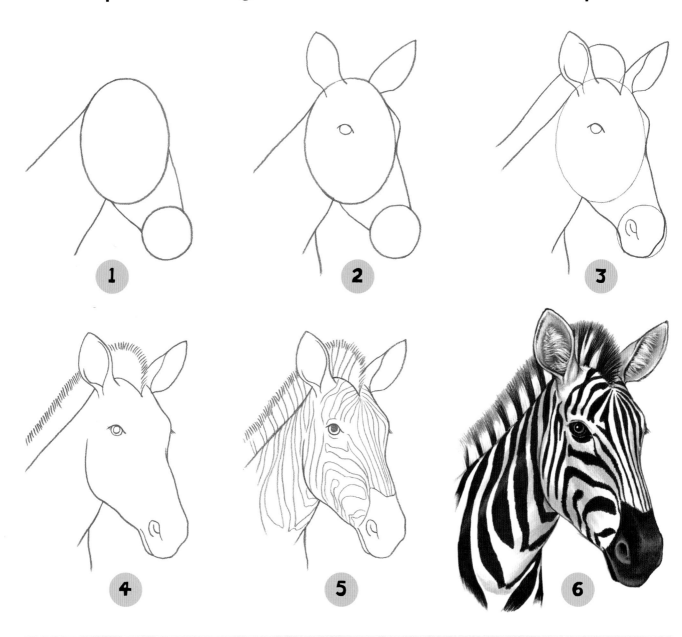

FUN FACT

Experts aren't exactly sure why zebras have stripes, but they think that the markings serve some sort of purpose. The stripes might help regulate temperature, or even confuse predators.